This Book Belongs To:

_____

_____

_____

For the weapons
of our warfare
are not carnal
but mighty in God
for pulling down
strongholds.

2 Corinthians 10:4

Date _____

Today is special because ...

I'm grateful for ...

My concerns or fears ...

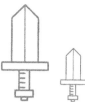

_____

_____

_____

_____

❖———————————————————————————————————————❖

Today I want to pray for ...

_____

_____

_____

_____

❖———————————————————————————————————————❖

God's Word says (get Mom or Dad's help if needed) ...

_____

_____

_____

Date _____

Today is special because ...

I'm grateful for ...

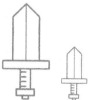

My concerns or fears ...

_____

_____

_____

_____

_____

Today I want to pray for ...

_____

_____

_____

_____

_____

God's Word says (get Mom or Dad's help if needed) ...

_____

_____

_____

Date _____

Today is special because ...

_____

_____

_____

_____

_____

I'm grateful for ...

_____

_____

_____

_____

_____

_____

_____

My concerns or fears ...

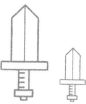

_____

_____

_____

_____

Today I want to pray for ...

_____

_____

_____

_____

God's Word says (get Mom or Dad's help if needed) ...

_____

_____

_____

Date _____

Today is special because ...

_____

_____

_____

_____

_____

I'm grateful for ...

_____

_____

_____

_____

_____

_____

_____

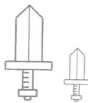

My concerns or fears ...

_____

_____

_____

_____

_____

Today I want to pray for ...

_____

_____

_____

_____

_____

God's Word says (get Mom or Dad's help if needed) ...

_____

_____

_____

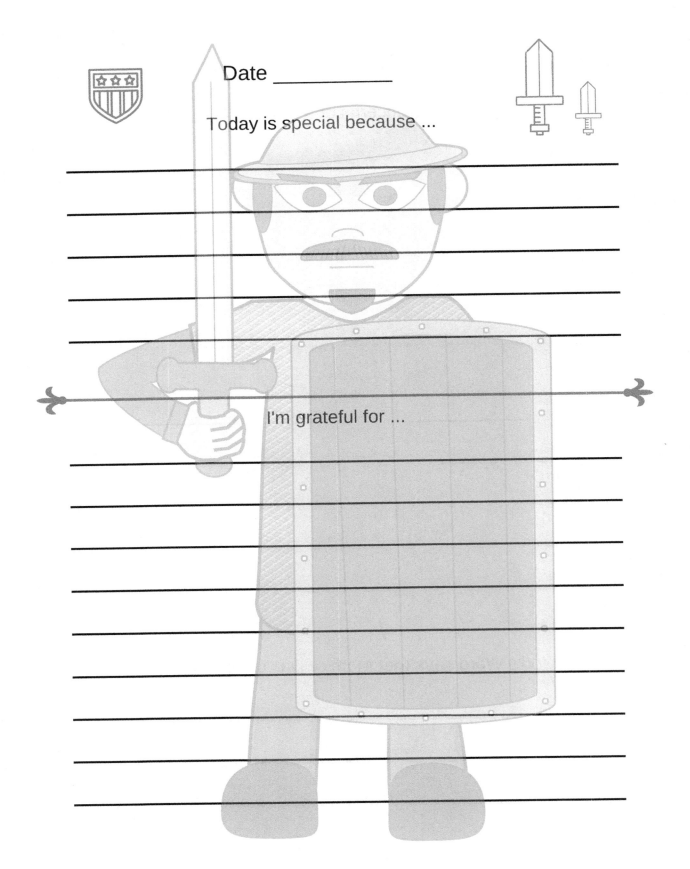

Date _____

Today is special because ...

I'm grateful for ...

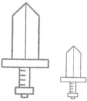

My concerns or fears ...

_____

_____

_____

_____

_____

Today I want to pray for ...

_____

_____

_____

_____

_____

God's Word says (get Mom or Dad's help if needed) ...

_____

_____

_____

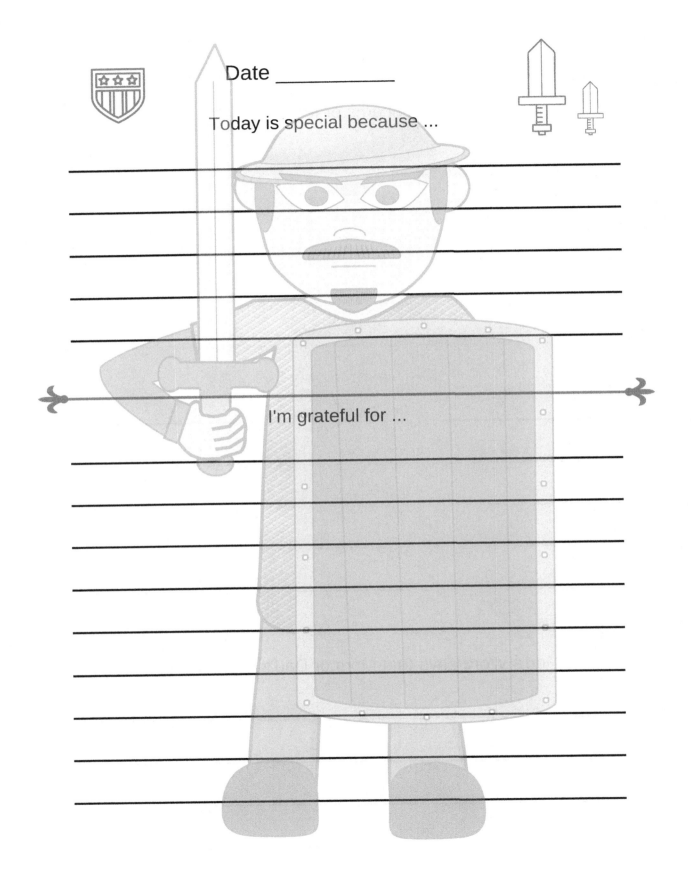

Date _____

Today is special because ...

I'm grateful for ...

My concerns or fears ...

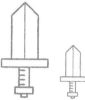

_____

_____

_____

_____

_____

Today I want to pray for ...

_____

_____

_____

_____

God's Word says (get Mom or Dad's help if needed) ...

_____

_____

_____

Date _____

Today is special because ...

I'm grateful for ...

My concerns or fears ...

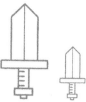

_____

_____

_____

_____

_____

Today I want to pray for ...

_____

_____

_____

_____

God's Word says (get Mom or Dad's help if needed) ...

_____

_____

_____

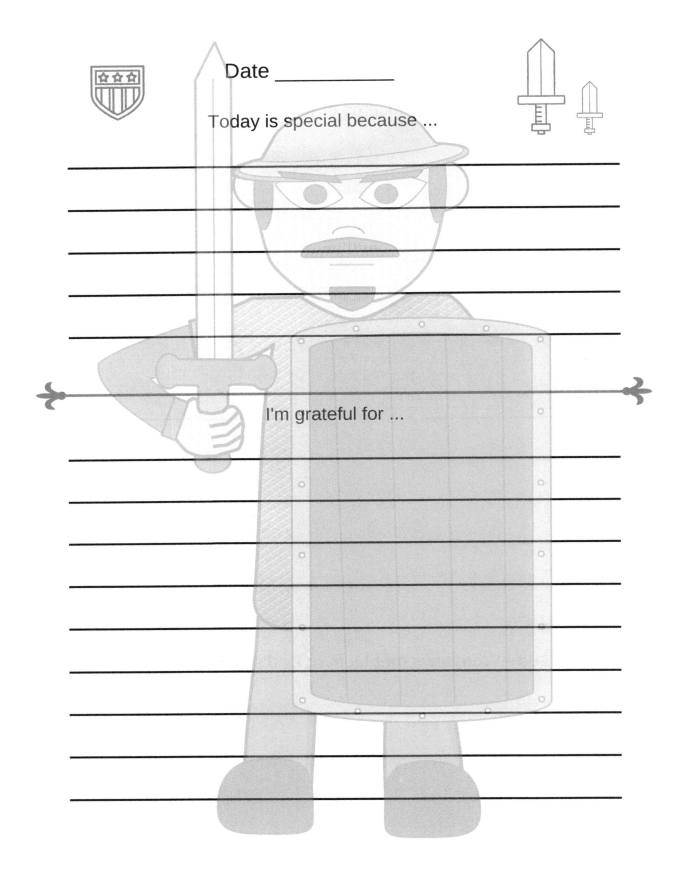

Date _____

Today is special because ...

I'm grateful for ...

My concerns or fears ...

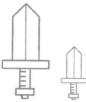

_____

_____

_____

_____

✦—————————————————————————————✦

Today I want to pray for ...

_____

_____

_____

_____

✦—————————————————————————————✦

God's Word says (get Mom or Dad's help if needed) ...

_____

_____

_____

Date _____

Today is special because ...

I'm grateful for ...

My concerns or fears ...

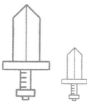

_____

_____

_____

_____

_____

Today I want to pray for ...

_____

_____

_____

_____

_____

God's Word says (get Mom or Dad's help if needed) ...

_____

_____

_____

Date _____

Today is special because ...

I'm grateful for ...

My concerns or fears ...

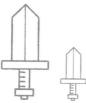

_____

_____

_____

_____

_____

Today I want to pray for ...

_____

_____

_____

_____

_____

God's Word says (get Mom or Dad's help if needed) ...

_____

_____

_____

Date _____

Today is special because ...

_____

_____

_____

_____

_____

I'm grateful for ...

_____

_____

_____

_____

_____

_____

_____

_____

My concerns or fears ...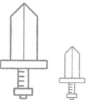

_____

_____

_____

_____

_____

Today I want to pray for ...

_____

_____

_____

_____

_____

God's Word says (get Mom or Dad's help if needed) ...

_____

_____

_____

Date _____

Today is special because ...

_____

_____

_____

_____

_____

I'm grateful for ...

_____

_____

_____

_____

_____

_____

_____

My concerns or fears ...

_____

_____

_____

_____

⫸————————————————————————————⫷

Today I want to pray for ...

_____

_____

_____

_____

⫸————————————————————————————⫷

God's Word says (get Mom or Dad's help if needed) ...

_____

_____

_____

Date _____

Today is special because ...

I'm grateful for ...

My concerns or fears ...

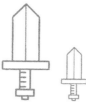

_____

_____

_____

_____

───

Today I want to pray for ...

_____

_____

_____

_____

_____

───

God's Word says (get Mom or Dad's help if needed) ...

_____

_____

_____

Date _____

Today is special because ...

I'm grateful for ...

My concerns or fears ...

Today I want to pray for ...

God's Word says (get Mom or Dad's help if needed) ...

Date _____

Today is special because ...

_____

_____

_____

_____

_____

I'm grateful for ...

_____

_____

_____

_____

_____

_____

_____

My concerns or fears ...

_____

_____

_____

_____

_____

Today I want to pray for ...

_____

_____

_____

_____

_____

God's Word says (get Mom or Dad's help if needed) ...

_____

_____

_____

Date _____

Today is special because ...

I'm grateful for ...

My concerns or fears ...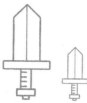

_____

_____

_____

_____

_____

Today I want to pray for ...

_____

_____

_____

_____

_____

God's Word says (get Mom or Dad's help if needed) ...

_____

_____

_____

Date _____

Today is special because ...

_____

_____

_____

_____

_____

I'm grateful for ...

_____

_____

_____

_____

_____

_____

_____

_____

My concerns or fears ...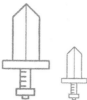

_____

_____

_____

_____

✦_____✦

Today I want to pray for ...

_____

_____

_____

_____

✦_____✦

God's Word says (get Mom or Dad's help if needed) ...

_____

_____

_____

Date _____

Today is special because ...

_____

_____

_____

_____

I'm grateful for ...

My concerns or fears ...

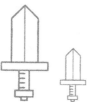

_____

_____

_____

_____

_____

Today I want to pray for ...

_____

_____

_____

_____

_____

God's Word says (get Mom or Dad's help if needed) ...

_____

_____

_____

Date _____

Today is special because ...

_____

_____

_____

_____

_____

I'm grateful for ...

_____

_____

_____

_____

_____

_____

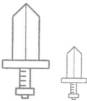

My concerns or fears ...

_____

_____

_____

_____

_____

Today I want to pray for ...

_____

_____

_____

_____

_____

God's Word says (get Mom or Dad's help if needed) ...

_____

_____

_____

Date _____

Today is special because ...

I'm grateful for ...

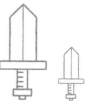

My concerns or fears ...

_____

_____

_____

_____

_____

Today I want to pray for ...

_____

_____

_____

_____

_____

God's Word says (get Mom or Dad's help if needed) ...

_____

_____

_____

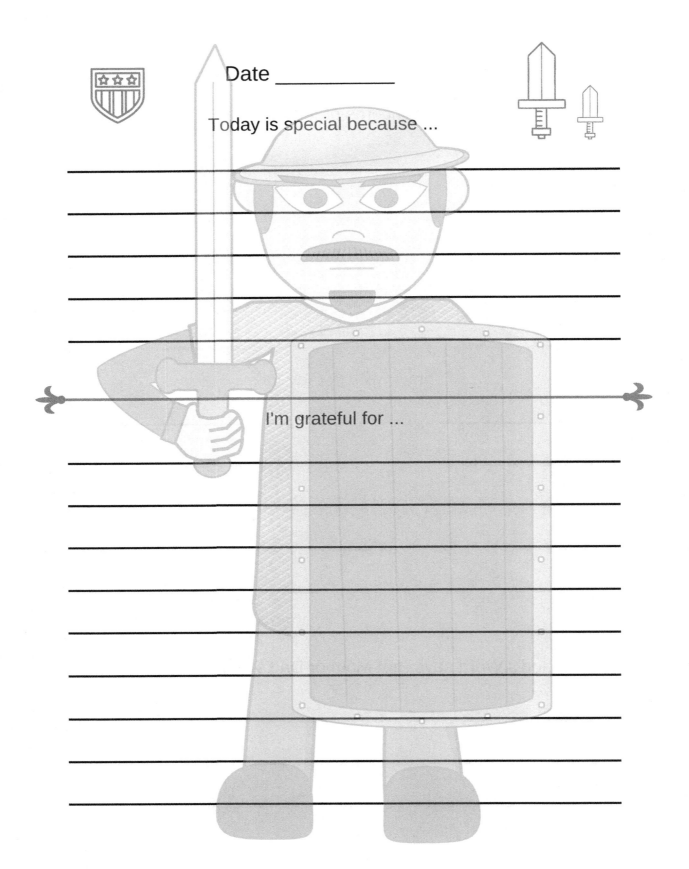

Date _____

Today is special because ...

I'm grateful for ...

My concerns or fears ...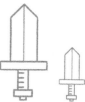

_____

_____

_____

_____

_____

Today I want to pray for ...

_____

_____

_____

_____

God's Word says (get Mom or Dad's help if needed) ...

_____

_____

_____

Date _____

Today is special because ...

I'm grateful for ...

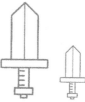

My concerns or fears ...

_____

_____

_____

_____

_____

Today I want to pray for ...

_____

_____

_____

_____

_____

God's Word says (get Mom or Dad's help if needed) ...

_____

_____

_____

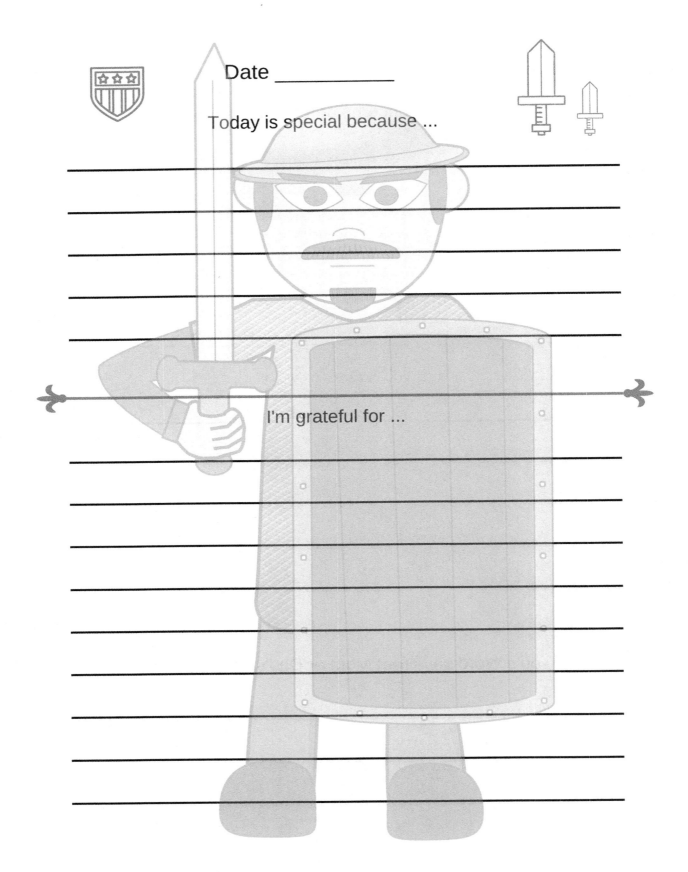

Date _____

Today is special because ...

_____

_____

_____

_____

I'm grateful for ...

_____

_____

_____

_____

_____

_____

_____

My concerns or fears ...

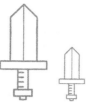

_____

_____

_____

_____

_____

Today I want to pray for ...

_____

_____

_____

_____

God's Word says (get Mom or Dad's help if needed) ...

_____

_____

_____

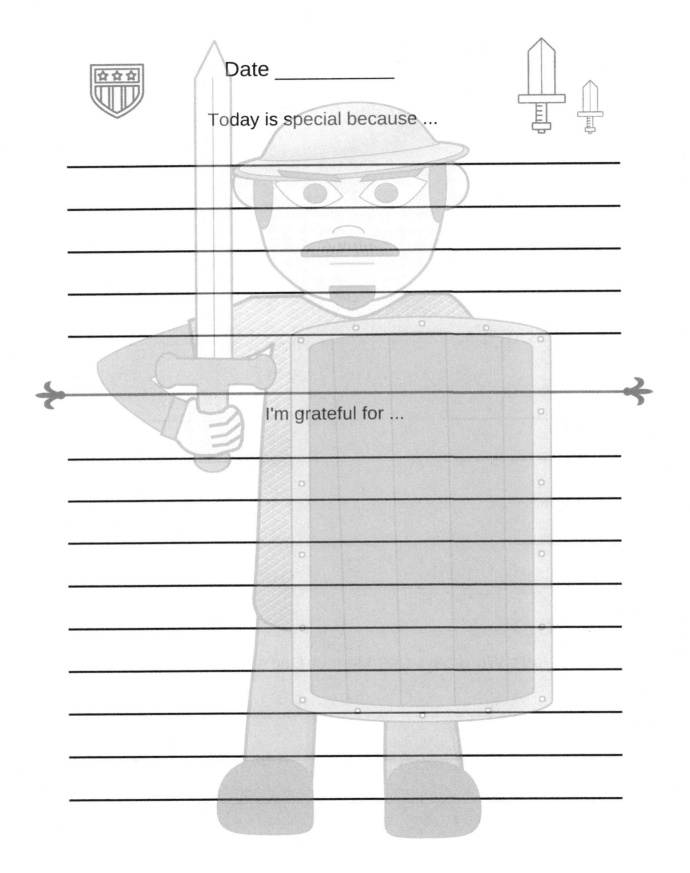

Date _____

Today is special because ...

_____

_____

_____

_____

_____

I'm grateful for ...

_____

_____

_____

_____

_____

_____

_____

_____

My concerns or fears ...

_____

_____

_____

_____

_____

Today I want to pray for ...

_____

_____

_____

_____

_____

God's Word says (get Mom or Dad's help if needed) ...

_____

_____

_____

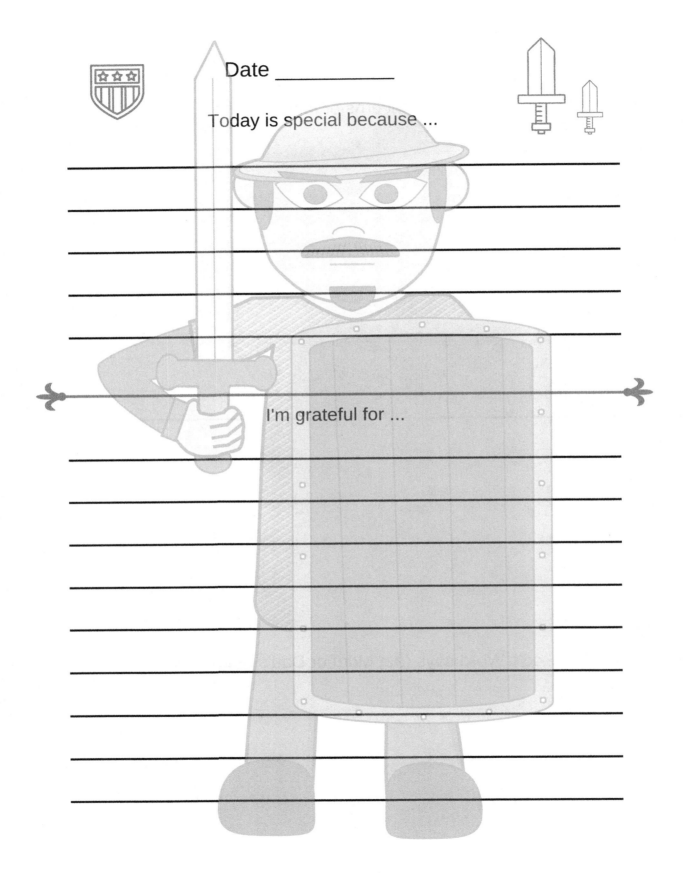

Date _____

Today is special because ...

I'm grateful for ...

My concerns or fears ...

_____

_____

_____

_____

_____

Today I want to pray for ...

_____

_____

_____

_____

God's Word says (get Mom or Dad's help if needed) ...

_____

_____

_____

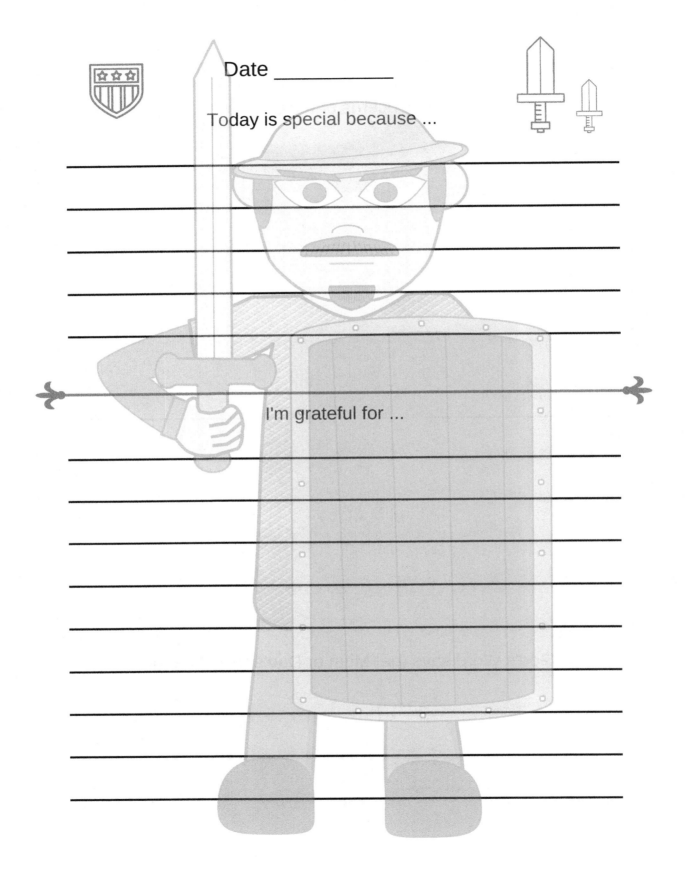

Date _____

Today is special because ...

I'm grateful for ...

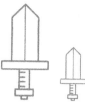

My concerns or fears ...

_____

_____

_____

_____

_____

Today I want to pray for ...

_____

_____

_____

_____

_____

God's Word says (get Mom or Dad's help if needed) ...

_____

_____

_____

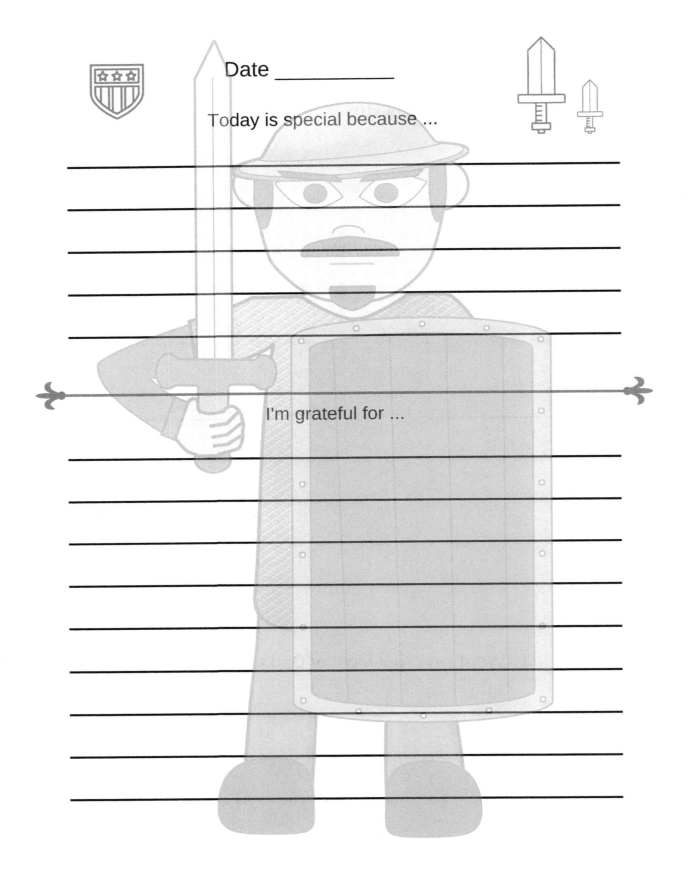

Date _____

Today is special because ...

_____

_____

_____

_____

I'm grateful for ...

_____

_____

_____

_____

_____

_____

My concerns or fears ...

_____

_____

_____

_____

✦————————————————————————————————✦

Today I want to pray for ...

_____

_____

_____

_____

✦————————————————————————————————✦

God's Word says (get Mom or Dad's help if needed) ...

_____

_____

_____

Date _____

Today is special because ...

I'm grateful for ...

My concerns or fears ...

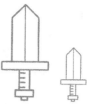

_____

_____

_____

_____

Today I want to pray for ...

_____

_____

_____

_____

God's Word says (get Mom or Dad's help if needed) ...

_____

_____

_____

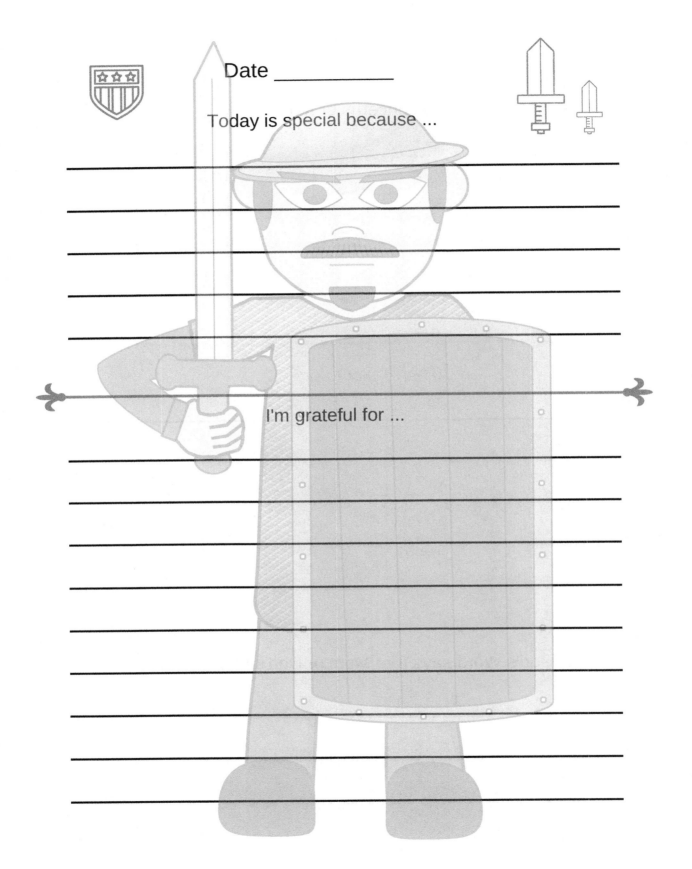

Date _____

Today is special because ...

I'm grateful for ...

My concerns or fears ...

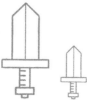

_____

_____

_____

_____

Today I want to pray for ...

_____

_____

_____

_____

God's Word says (get Mom or Dad's help if needed) ...

_____

_____

_____

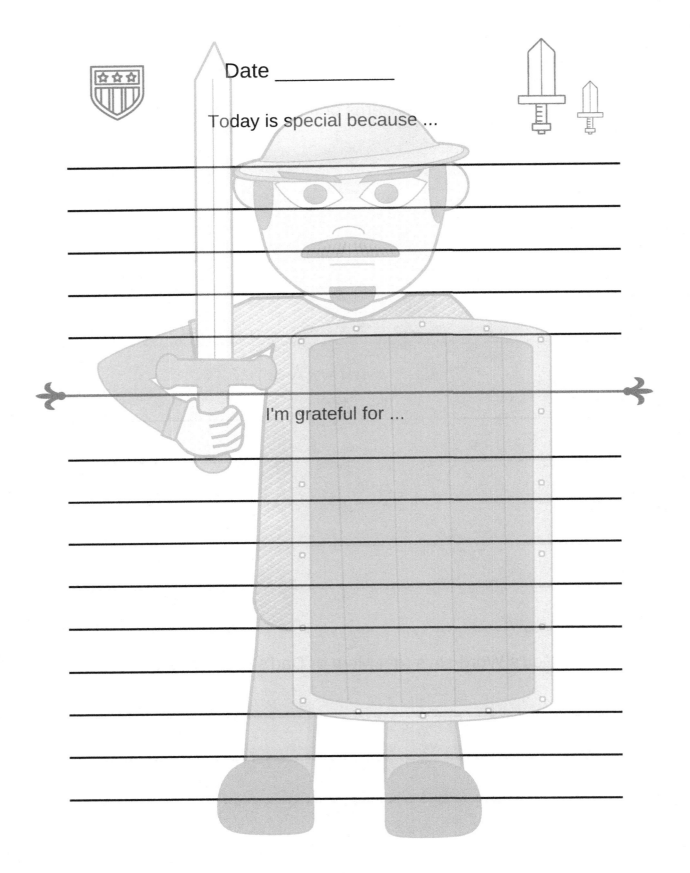

Date _____

Today is special because ...

_____
_____
_____
_____
_____

I'm grateful for ...

_____
_____
_____
_____
_____
_____
_____
_____

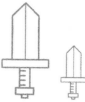

My concerns or fears ...

_____

_____

_____

_____

_____

Today I want to pray for ...

_____

_____

_____

_____

_____

God's Word says (get Mom or Dad's help if needed) ...

_____

_____

_____

Date _____

Today is special because ...

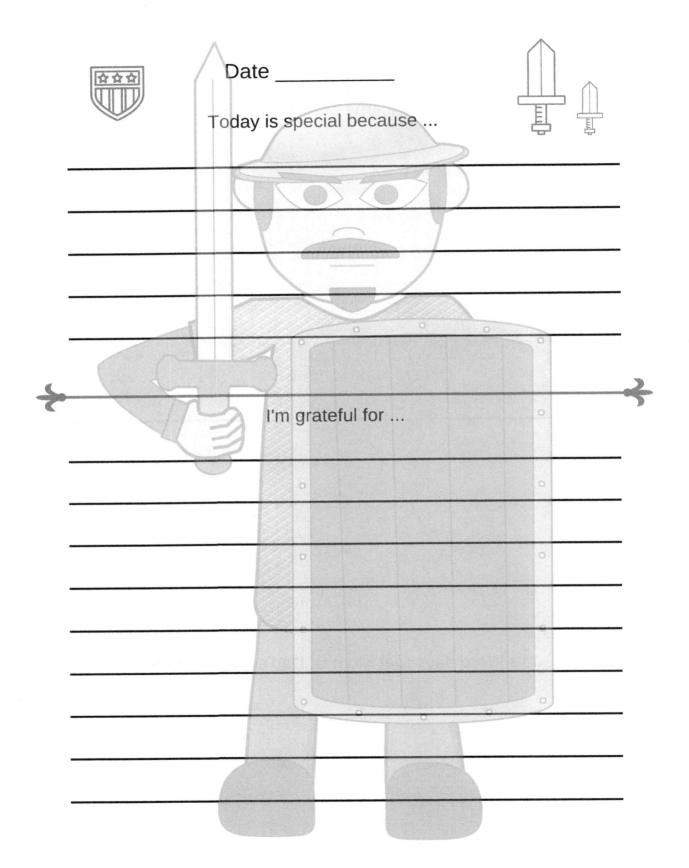

I'm grateful for ...

My concerns or fears ...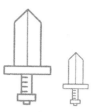

_____

_____

_____

_____

Today I want to pray for ...

_____

_____

_____

_____

God's Word says (get Mom or Dad's help if needed) ...

_____

_____

_____

Date _____

Today is special because ...

I'm grateful for ...

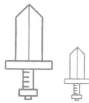

My concerns or fears ...

_____

_____

_____

_____

_____

Today I want to pray for ...

_____

_____

_____

_____

_____

God's Word says (get Mom or Dad's help if needed) ...

_____

_____

_____

Date _____

Today is special because ...

I'm grateful for ...

My concerns or fears ...

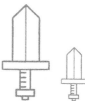

_____

_____

_____

_____

_____

Today I want to pray for ...

_____

_____

_____

_____

God's Word says (get Mom or Dad's help if needed) ...

_____

_____

_____

Date _____

Today is special because ...

I'm grateful for ...

My concerns or fears ...

Today I want to pray for ...

God's Word says (get Mom or Dad's help if needed) ...

Date _____

Today is special because ...

I'm grateful for ...

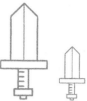

My concerns or fears ...

_____

_____

_____

_____

_____

Today I want to pray for ...

_____

_____

_____

_____

_____

God's Word says (get Mom or Dad's help if needed) ...

_____

_____

_____

Date _____

Today is special because ...

_____

_____

_____

_____

_____

I'm grateful for ...

_____

_____

_____

_____

_____

_____

_____

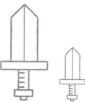

My concerns or fears ...

_____

_____

_____

_____

Today I want to pray for ...

_____

_____

_____

_____

God's Word says (get Mom or Dad's help if needed) ...

_____

_____

_____

Date _____

Today is special because ...

I'm grateful for ...

My concerns or fears ...

_____

_____

_____

_____

_____

Today I want to pray for ...

_____

_____

_____

_____

_____

God's Word says (get Mom or Dad's help if needed) ...

_____

_____

_____

Date _____

Today is special because ...

_____
_____
_____
_____
_____

I'm grateful for ...

_____
_____
_____
_____
_____
_____
_____

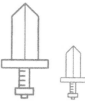

My concerns or fears ...

_____

_____

_____

_____

_____

Today I want to pray for ...

_____

_____

_____

_____

God's Word says (get Mom or Dad's help if needed) ...

_____

_____

_____

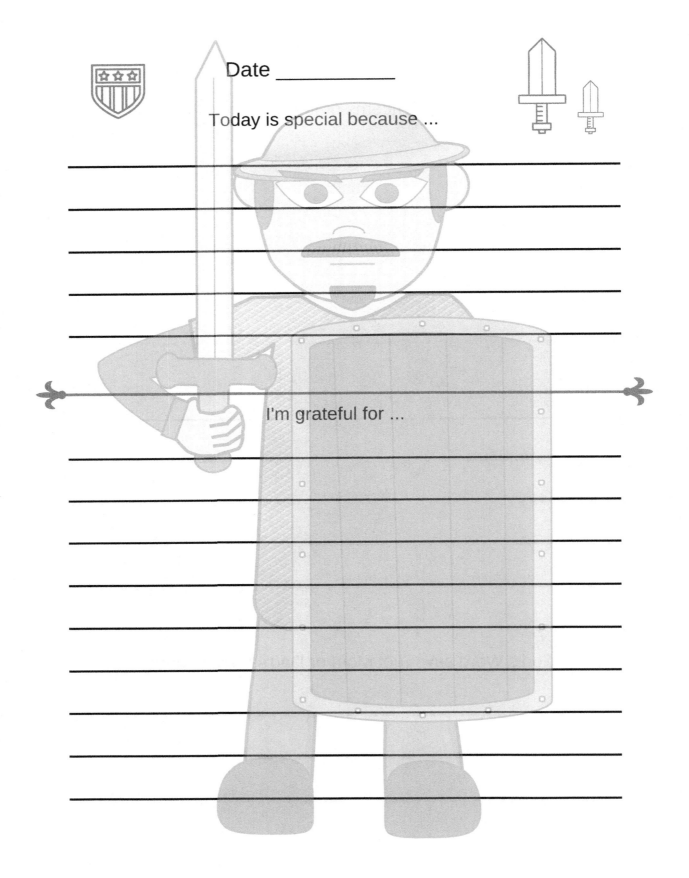

Date _____

Today is special because ...

_____

_____

_____

_____

_____

I'm grateful for ...

_____

_____

_____

_____

_____

_____

_____

_____

My concerns or fears ...

_____

_____

_____

_____

❖———————————————————————————————❖

Today I want to pray for ...

_____

_____

_____

_____

❖———————————————————————————————❖

God's Word says (get Mom or Dad's help if needed) ...

_____

_____

_____

Date _____

Today is special because ...

I'm grateful for ...

My concerns or fears ...

_____

_____

_____

_____

Today I want to pray for ...

_____

_____

_____

_____

God's Word says (get Mom or Dad's help if needed) ...

_____

_____

_____

Date _____

Today is special because ...

I'm grateful for ...

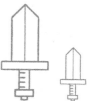

My concerns or fears ...

_____

_____

_____

_____

_____

Today I want to pray for ...

_____

_____

_____

_____

_____

God's Word says (get Mom or Dad's help if needed) ...

_____

_____

_____

Date _____

Today is special because ...

I'm grateful for ...

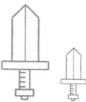

My concerns or fears ...

_____

_____

_____

_____

_____

Today I want to pray for ...

_____

_____

_____

_____

God's Word says (get Mom or Dad's help if needed) ...

_____

_____

_____

Date _____

Today is special because ...

I'm grateful for ...

My concerns or fears ...

_____

_____

_____

_____

Today I want to pray for ...

_____

_____

_____

_____

God's Word says (get Mom or Dad's help if needed) ...

_____

_____

_____

Date _____

Today is special because ...

I'm grateful for ...

My concerns or fears ...

_____

_____

_____

_____

_____

Today I want to pray for ...

_____

_____

_____

_____

_____

God's Word says (get Mom or Dad's help if needed) ...

_____

_____

_____

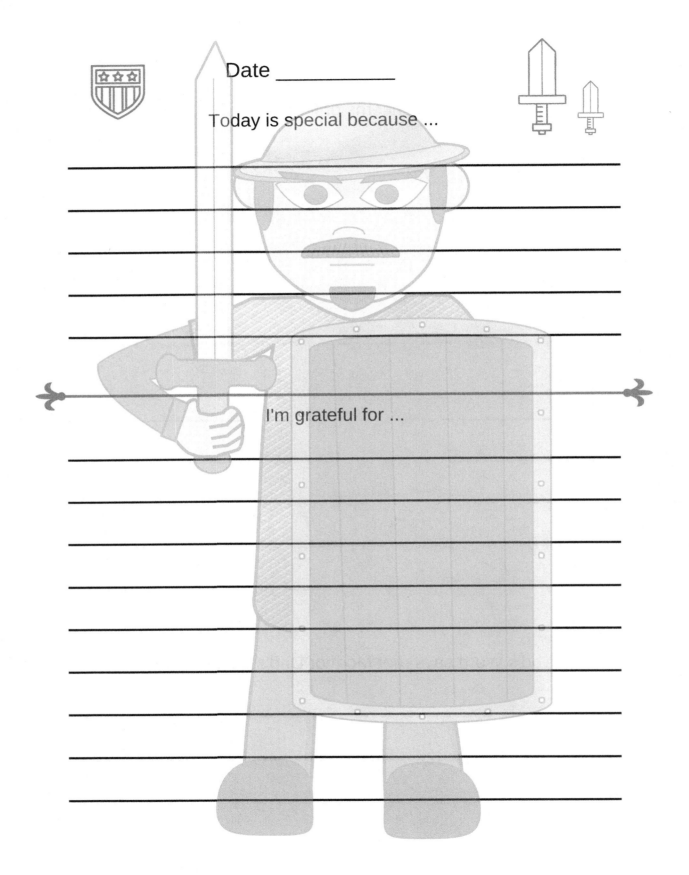

Date _____

Today is special because ...

I'm grateful for ...

My concerns or fears ...

_____

_____

_____

_____

Today I want to pray for ...

_____

_____

_____

_____

God's Word says (get Mom or Dad's help if needed) ...

_____

_____

_____

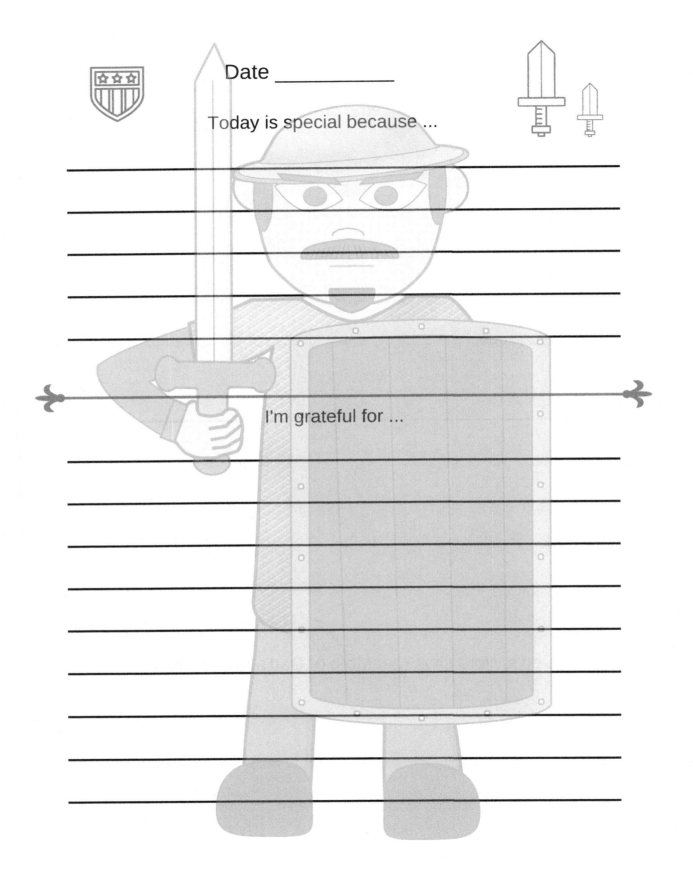

Date _____

Today is special because ...

_____

_____

_____

_____

I'm grateful for ...

_____

_____

_____

_____

_____

_____

My concerns or fears ...

_____

_____

_____

_____

Today I want to pray for ...

_____

_____

_____

_____

God's Word says (get Mom or Dad's help if needed) ...

_____

_____

_____

Date _____

Today is special because ...

_____

_____

_____

_____

_____

I'm grateful for ...

_____

_____

_____

_____

_____

_____

_____

My concerns or fears ...

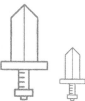

_____

_____

_____

_____

❧━━━━━━━━━━━━━━━━━━━━━━━━━━━━❧

Today I want to pray for ...

_____

_____

_____

_____

❧━━━━━━━━━━━━━━━━━━━━━━━━━━━━❧

God's Word says (get Mom or Dad's help if needed) ...

_____

_____

_____

Date _____

Today is special because ...

I'm grateful for ...

My concerns or fears ...

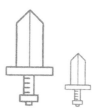

_____

_____

_____

_____

⚜—————————————————————————⚜

Today I want to pray for ...

_____

_____

_____

_____

⚜—————————————————————————⚜

God's Word says (get Mom or Dad's help if needed) ...

_____

_____

_____

Date _____

Today is special because ...

I'm grateful for ...

My concerns or fears ...

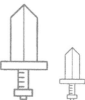

_____

_____

_____

_____

_____

Today I want to pray for ...

_____

_____

_____

_____

_____

God's Word says (get Mom or Dad's help if needed) ...

_____

_____

_____

Date _____

Today is special because ...

_____

_____

_____

_____

_____

I'm grateful for ...

_____

_____

_____

_____

_____

_____

_____

My concerns or fears ...

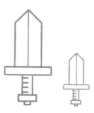

_____

_____

_____

_____

Today I want to pray for ...

_____

_____

_____

_____

God's Word says (get Mom or Dad's help if needed) ...

_____

_____

_____

Date _____

Today is special because ...

I'm grateful for ...

My concerns or fears ...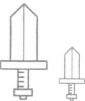

_____

_____

_____

_____

_____

Today I want to pray for ...

_____

_____

_____

_____

_____

God's Word says (get Mom or Dad's help if needed) ...

_____

_____

_____

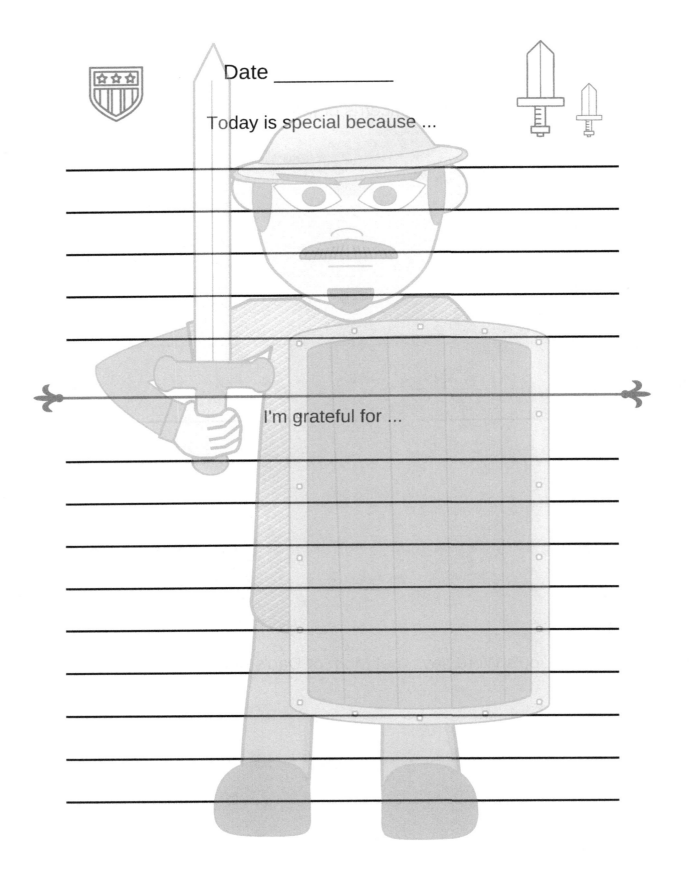

Date _____

Today is special because ...

I'm grateful for ...

My concerns or fears ...

_____

_____

_____

_____

_____

Today I want to pray for ...

_____

_____

_____

_____

_____

God's Word says (get Mom or Dad's help if needed) ...

_____

_____

_____

Date _____

Today is special because ...

I'm grateful for ...

My concerns or fears ...

_____

_____

_____

_____

Today I want to pray for ...

_____

_____

_____

_____

God's Word says (get Mom or Dad's help if needed) ...

_____

_____

_____

Date _____

Today is special because ...

I'm grateful for ...

My concerns or fears ...

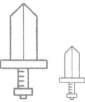

_____

_____

_____

_____

Today I want to pray for ...

_____

_____

_____

_____

God's Word says (get Mom or Dad's help if needed) ...

_____

_____

_____

Date _____

Today is special because ...

I'm grateful for ...

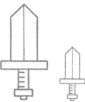

My concerns or fears ...

_____

_____

_____

_____

_____

Today I want to pray for ...

_____

_____

_____

_____

_____

God's Word says (get Mom or Dad's help if needed) ...

_____

_____

_____

Date _____

Today is special because ...

I'm grateful for ...

My concerns or fears ...

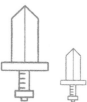

_____

_____

_____

_____

_____

Today I want to pray for ...

_____

_____

_____

_____

_____

God's Word says (get Mom or Dad's help if needed) ...

_____

_____

_____

Date _____

Today is special because ...

I'm grateful for ...

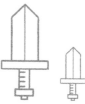

My concerns or fears ...

_____

_____

_____

_____

_____

Today I want to pray for ...

_____

_____

_____

_____

_____

God's Word says (get Mom or Dad's help if needed) ...

_____

_____

_____

Date _____

Today is special because ...

I'm grateful for ...

My concerns or fears ...

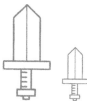

_____

_____

_____

_____

_____

Today I want to pray for ...

_____

_____

_____

_____

_____

God's Word says (get Mom or Dad's help if needed) ...

_____

_____

_____

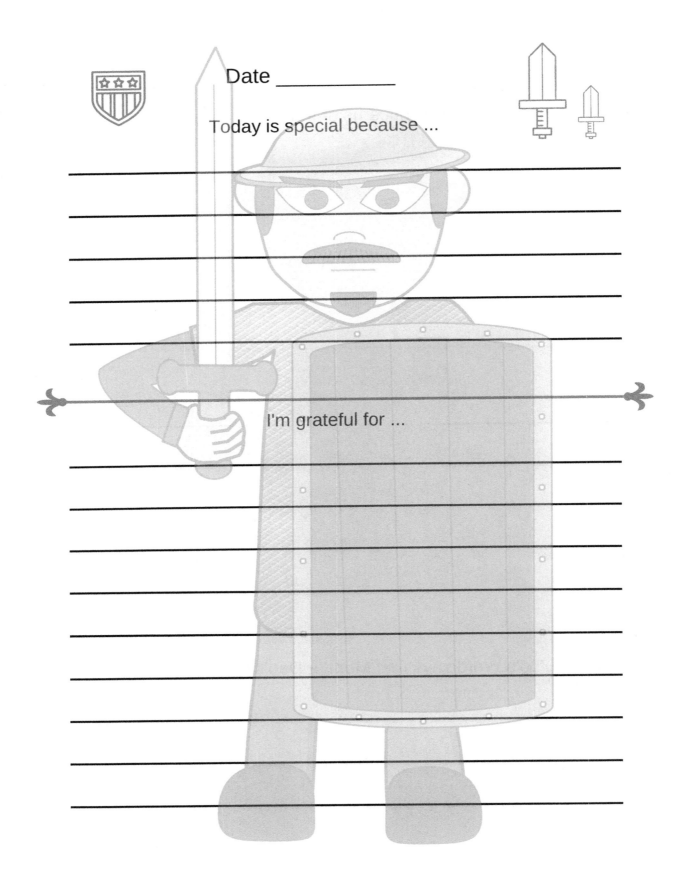

Date _____

Today is special because ...

I'm grateful for ...

My concerns or fears ...

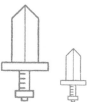

_____

_____

_____

_____

_____

Today I want to pray for ...

_____

_____

_____

_____

_____

God's Word says (get Mom or Dad's help if needed) ...

_____

_____

_____

Date _____

Today is special because ...

I'm grateful for ...

My concerns or fears ...

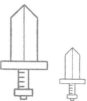

_____

_____

_____

_____

Today I want to pray for ...

_____

_____

_____

_____

God's Word says (get Mom or Dad's help if needed) ...

_____

_____

_____